Claire Llewellyn

Contents

At a Safari Park

In Africa there are many **safari parks**. Safari parks are very big and they have lots of different animals in them.

Guides work at the safari parks. Guides take people out in **jeeps** to see the animals. This is called going on safari.

Looking for Lions

Safari guides take people to look for lions. Lions are big cats with long teeth. They are hunters. They hunt and kill many animals in the park.

The guides know where to find lions. They know lions are often near water. They sleep under trees in the day, when it is too hot for them to hunt.

Fact

Male lions have a **mane** around their face.

The guides stop the jeep when they see a group of lions. A group of lions has only one or two male lions. Most of the lions in a group are females or **cubs**.

Fact

Lions live together in groups called **prides**.

Safari guides take people out at night too. That is when lions hunt. The lions kill an animal, and then they **feed** on it. The males feed first, then the females. The cubs feed last!

Fact

Lions hunt for food at night.

Looking for Elephants

Safari guides take people to look for elephants. Elephants are the biggest animals in the park. They have very big ears and a long trunk.

The guides know where to find elephants. They know that female elephants live in small groups. In the day, they often sleep under a tree.

Fact

An elephant's trunk has no bones.

The guides stop the jeep when they see a group of elephants. People like to see the elephants near water. They like to see the baby elephants play in the water.

Fact

Elephants can drink 8 litres of water at a time.

Safari guides often take people to see the elephants eat. Elephants feed in the day and at night. They feed on trees and grass.

Fact

Elephants feed on leaves.

Looking for Hippos

Safari guides take people to look for hippos. Hippos are very big animals. They are about as long as a jeep.

The guides know where to find hippos. They know that hippos are often in water. The water keeps the hippos from getting too hot. People can't see the hippos very well in the water. The hippos often go under the water. Then people can't see them at all!

Fact

The name *hippopotamus* means "river horse".

The guides stop the jeep when they see a group of hippos. Most of the hippos in a group are females or babies. The biggest hippos are males.

Fact

Hippos have very big mouths.

Safari guides often take people to see hippos at night. The hippos come out of the water at night. They feed on grass.

Fact
Hippos feed at night.

Looking for Giraffes

Safari guides take people to look for giraffes. Giraffes are the tallest animals in the park. They have very long legs and a very long neck.

The guides know where to find giraffes. They often find a group of giraffes feeding on trees. A group of giraffes has male, female and baby giraffes.

Fact

A giraffe's neck has seven bones in it, just as ours does!

The guides stop the jeep when they see giraffes. Male giraffes are taller than the females. A male giraffe can feed on very tall trees.

Fact

Male giraffes can grow to be 5 metres tall.

Giraffes are often hunted by lions. But giraffes can kick lions with their feet. They can run very fast too.

Fact

Giraffes can run up to 35 miles per hour.

Looking for Ostriches

Safari guides take people to look for ostriches. Ostriches are the biggest birds in the park. They have long legs and a long neck.

The guides know where to find ostriches. They know that ostriches live in small groups. The guides know that ostriches feed on grass too.

Fact

Ostriches are the biggest birds in the world.

The guides stop the jeep when they see ostriches. People often see a male ostrich with a female. The male and female ostriches often have babies at their feet.

Fact

Male ostriches are mostly black. Females are mostly brown.

Ostriches are big birds, so other animals do not often kill them. Ostriches can run very fast too. And they have big feet, so they can kick very hard!

Fact

Ostriches can run up to 40 miles per hour.

Glossary

cub	a very young lion
feed	to eat something
jeep	a four-wheeled vehicle that can travel over rough ground.
mane	the long, thick hair around the head of a male lion
pride	a group or family of lions
safari guide	a person who leads groups of people through a safari park
safari park	a park where people can see animals in the wild